Bibliographic information published by the German National Library:

The German National Library lists this publication in the National Bibliography; detailed bibliographic data are available on the Internet at http://dnb.dnb.de .

Imprint:

Copyright © 2017 GRIN Verlag, Open Publishing GmbH
Print and binding: Books on Demand GmbH, Norderstedt Germany
ISBN: 9783668507630

This book at GRIN:

http://www.grin.com/en/e-book/371790/a-look-at-improvement-possibilities-of-online-dating-considering-personal

Jessica Möller

A Look at Improvement Possibilities of Online Dating Considering Personal Interests and Fandoms

GRIN Publishing

GRIN - Your knowledge has value

Since its foundation in 1998, GRIN has specialized in publishing academic texts by students, college teachers and other academics as e-book and printed book. The website www.grin.com is an ideal platform for presenting term papers, final papers, scientific essays, dissertations and specialist books.

Visit us on the internet:

http://www.grin.com/

http://www.facebook.com/grincom

http://www.twitter.com/grin_com

A Look at Improvement Possibilities of **Online Dating** Considering Personal Interests and Fandoms

2017-06-31

BMSB3310 Market Research

Assignment, graded 1.3 ($\approx$A)

Jessica Möller

Content

1.) Executive Summary

This report provides an analysis and evaluation of the current online dating market, the needs of its users and possibilities for its improvement, especially, but not exclusively, concerning the inclusion of interests and fandoms.

For the collection of data a survey has been conducted asking students of Stralsund University of Applied Science questions concerning their experiences, opinions and suggestions concerning this topic.

Results of the data analyzed show that although the most used online dating services are based on matching through looks, this is with a high probability more likely due to the network effect (i.a. joining service with already big user base) than to the costumers belief in this method, since character traits and similar interests seem to be valued more and play an important role in their life.

The assignment also goes more into detail about what these interests are and how they are manifested, forming the basis for an improved online dating experience.

It is advised to use to gained knowledge about potential costumers interests and provide them with an improved possibility to present themselves to others online, including a more sophisticated profile. Entering the niche market of fandom based online dating is also a possibility that, according to the authors findings, might prove profitable.

Even though the market of online dating platforms is increasing and well off, it might proof to be important to listen to the needs of existing and potential users, to maintain and gain costumers over the following years.

1.) Research Analysis

2.1) Objective of the Survey

The traditional way of meeting others has changed for a considerable amount of people recently. *Dating apps and websites* have increased their importance especially for young people in the last 5 years and are predicted to grow even more. (Stewart, Caitlin; 2016) With 8.4 Mio active users in Germany alone the success of this business model is obvious. (Statista, 2015) There are used to make new acquaintances or even to find a partner. But most focus more on looks (e.g. Tinder,

Lovoo) or careers (e.g. ElitePartner) than on interests, what, in the authors opinion, makes it harder to find someone that matches the user and often creates frustration.

Most *online dating services* function on a very simple principle. The user creates a profile, free or on charge, where they present themselves with a picture and some basic information, for example a brief summary sentence. Then they are shown profiles of other users of the preferred gender and get to choose if they are interested in them, a common method for this is "swiping" pictures. If they express interest, they get to initiate a chat.

While the, up to this point, most successful players of this market work with values and characteristics that could be considered rather superficial, there might also be a strong market for a service of this kind focusing more on personality and similarities and present an easier way to match users based on those.

In this survey the author tried to get more precise idea about what users are looking for in an online dating service, what they are interested in when looking for a partner and what role their fandoms play in this. *Fandoms* can be described as the interest in a particular creation or activity, like a sport or a TV series, and the community and culture arising from it.

With this information, the possibilities of entering a niche market of the online dating industry or improving the already existing concepts, are examined for business porpoises like enhancing user experience and improving costumer loyalty, as well as gaining new users through this. This scientific writing will enquire into following hypothesizes: *There is a niche market for a fandom based dating apps.*
And: *Users prefer character over looks and therefor want more possibilities to find out about it faster*

2.2) Project plan

First, critical aspects like research design, methodology, target group and sample size were defined. This constructed the basis of the research.

The projects main task was the creation and analysis of a survey about online and real life dating behavior, interests and opinions. Therefore assumptions about the target group and the online dating market in general had to be taken into

3

consideration to create questions with to most precise possible outcome for the porpoise. This also included a prior research considering existing services and statistics.

The timespan of creation and inspection was about a week, after which the online survey was accessible to the selected target group from 27th May – 27th April,

project steps / tasks
choosing of methods, target group etc.
assembling of general assumptions
creating of survey questions and choosing of platform
distribution of survey (Pressestelle)
survey time (about 1 month)
analysis (findings, interdependecies...)
gathering of most important findings and their effects
assignment

after which the analysis in combination to further secondary research could take place. It included the emphasis on important findings and their value for business porpoises. The creation of a scientific writing could be processed until the official submission date of 14th July.

2.3) Research Design

For this market research the use of primary methods, with secondary research only to prepare the primary research and better understand its findings, seemed appropriate. The data was collected via an online survey hosted by umfrageonline.com, allowing the use of different kinds of questions like scales, multiple choice etc and being available to the target group independently from their schedule and location. A questionnaire appeared to be the most efficient tool, for it allows to collect anonym opinions of a larger sample.

The survey consisted of 22 questions, with some being very short and some more detailed, divided into the topics of "online dating", "dating in general", "fandoms and other interests" as well as demographic questions. It was conducted once in a time span of a month, with most answers being given within the first 3 days. The comparable long time span was chosen because of the distribution method.

Links to the survey were sent to all students of Stralsund University of Applied Science via email. Of the potential about 2227 test subjects (Stralsund University of Applied Science, 2015) 166 answered the survey, leading to a response rate of

4

7.5%, which comes close to average response rates of 10-15% for external surveys. (Fryrear, Andrea; 2015), even more if students at a semester abroad or practical semester are taken into consideration, who may check their university mails less frequent. With this sample size, an average failure of 3,88% is accepted, varying depending on question.

Despite this mixture of cluster and quota sampling (students of one location) a certain randomness is guaranteed due to high number of possible participants and no bias by degree course or age. However, overall it is a more selective than random sample.

Sampling students from one particular university is not exclusively due to the availability of contact data, but foremost because of the relevance of the topic to this specific group of consumers. Young people between the age of 18 and 32 (actual ages of participants) are the main target group for many online dating service providers and, according to a research by Pew Research Center, have the highest percentages of people who have used online dating, with 27% for the age group 18-24 and 22% for 25-34 year-olds. (Anderson, M.; Smith; A.; 2016)
The choice of Stralsund, as a smaller town with 57,525 inhabitants (Hansestadt Stralsund, 2015), is important to this study, concerning the smaller possibilities to meet someone through lesser known online dating services.

2.4) Methodology

The elaborate survey contains different kinds of questions. There are simple yes-or-no questions to capture simple facts, but also more detailed multiple choice questions that most of the time offer room for individual answers, as well as scales, ranks and open questions. This mix of different types was supposed to motivate the participants to finish the rather detailed questionnaire and also provides more diverse data to work with. The full questionnaire can be found in the appendix.

To analyze the resulting data, most often simple proportions in percentages were used, comparing different answers to one, or interrelations between various questions. Also widely used in this are means and standard deviations from the mean, there appeared to necessity to also include the median in the final analysis.

5

Since it is the goal of the assignment to assess to behavior and opinions of a certain target group, but also of smaller groups in between, there were often comparative means applied.

2.5) Limitations of the report

The value of the findings are limited due to a number of participants (166) and the rather selective sampling, using students of one single university. While a clear pattern in the answers was observed early on, after a small number of participants, the results could vary on different locations, different age groups, as well as in other fields of work or education.

While the average accepted failure of 3.88% seems to be an acceptable value, this is only an average of some of the questions asked, assuming the percentage of answers being split 50:50 and the question being answered by all 166 participants. Other questions, like question 3, have even better values (3.6%), while question 18 differs much from the norm with 4,85% accepted failure, considering 102 respondents and values of 59,8% to 40,2%.

Other inaccuracies may have occurred due to unfinished questionnaires. Some early terminations were caused by the survey not being available for a short period of time in the beginning phase due to technical errors, but also the length of the survey might have caused participants not to finish.

2.) Research and Results

3.1) Survey and Participants

As stated before, the questionnaire consisting of 22 questions was answered by 166 university students of which 106 finished the whole survey. Only considering answers of completely finished questionnaires does not influence the outcome by more than a few percent, so all answers given will be taken into consideration.

The participants were between 18 and 32 years old with a mean of 23. There is a slight majority of female participants, but since there are only minimal differences between the answers of different genders, which will be discussed later, this is not influencing the outcome dramatically. There is also no age difference between different genders.

Even if Stralsund University of Applied Science is focused on internationality, it is not possible to distinguish between opinions based on their nationality since 97% said Germany is their home country.

3.2) Existing online dating services

3.2.1) Most successful services

Before assessing the outcome of the survey, a small overview about the some of the most successful online dating services used in Germany will be given. The mentioned apps and websites are also the most widely used and known by the sample. This will help to understand opinions, experiences and suggestions expressed in the survey, as well as the market in general.

The app most used by the participants is *Lovoo*, with 65 Million users worldwide (Lovoo, 2016). Over half of the participants that had tried online dating in there life had done so via Lovoo, an app with a simple principle: Looking at someone's photograph and deciding based on attractiveness if they want to meet that person. This free service made in Dresden, Germany has been used by 32% of students. Part of this success could be due to the matching algorithm; the technique used to pair users together (stated by 48% of users), but also the high amount of users in the area, which was rated as especially good by about 2 of every 3 Lovoo users.

Tinder has made the "swiping" of pictures famous and is known for it by 95% percent of young people. It has even 1.6 Billion profiles and matches the user by facebook friends, facebook added interests and mainly via swiping. (N-TV, 2016) The dependence on a facebook account has been criticized by participants of the survey; still over a third of them uses or used this app. It is free, but also has some additional pay options and has been developed by InterActiveCorp, New York, USA.

It´s ratings for design (71% of users), amount of other users in the area (83%) and matching algorithm (66%) excel the ones of their competitors, which explains why 41% of the online dating users and 23% of all students in the sample have already tried it. But still less than 1/5 like the way they can present themselves to others on this app.

Other highly used apps include Badoo (used by 10%) and Candidate (used by 8%), but do not come close to the success of Lovoo and Tinder. This might be highly influenced by the limited inhabitant number of the target location. Users seem to consider the amount of other users nearby too small.

The dating services participants could comment to a list of 8 widely known apps and websites. There were noticeably high differences between recognition and use, for example for Parship and ElitePartner, which were known to 90-92% but did not appeal to more than 0-4% of our target group.

Participants have also added Joyclub, Lesarion and Once to the default list themselves, proving a strong interest in these services. Since there is only few data on them, a real analysis seems unnecessary.

	know	use		use (of users of online dating)
Tinder	95%	26%		41%
Lovoo	90%	32%		52%
Parship	92%	4%		7%
eHarmony	38%	4%		7%
OKCupid	32%	7%		11%
ElitePartner	90%	0%		0%
Badoo	44%	10%		15%
Candidate	29%	8%		13%
Joyclub	1%	1%		1%
Lesarion	1%	1%		1%
Once	1%	1%		1%

3.2.2) Niche products

Since one of the hypothesizes deals with the correlation of fandom and dating there will be a brief overview on online dating services that specialize in this niche and a possible reason why they have not had a breakthrough yet.

Existing fandom, interest and identity based dating services all specialize on one certain aspect (dating for Star Trek fans, for horse lovers, for Christians etc.), but do not allow to present the user as more than one thing primarily. Over 1000 of these webpages belong to Online Connections Inc., a company based in Florida, USA.

(OnlineConnections Inc., unknown year) Since they all are very specific of course there is only a limited user base.

3.3) Dating Behavior

3.3.1) Experiences

It appears that the majority (57%) of college students has already tried online dating at least once in their life but only slightly more than one third of these people has actually succeeded in finding a friend, partner or similar via such services. However, an impressive proportion of 70% knows at least one other person that has found what there were looking for in online dating, with only 15% being sure that they know no one who has met someone that way.

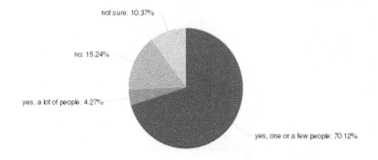

Do you know someone else who has succeeded in finding a partner/friend/etc. on an online dating platform?

The top ways to find potential love interests can still be considered traditional. 87% of the participants stated that they get to know their dates through friends, with only an ignorable amount less of them dating people they know from work, school or university. Hobbies seem to be a significant source for finding a partner or date as well, according to 61% of the sample. Online dating is on its way to gain importance for young people, still less than 30% consider it as a mean to get a date, which, nether the less, is used more than talking to strangers e.g. on the street in which only 25% said they succeeded in. 8% additionally named parties as a way they met someone

3.3.2) Preferences

The participants were asked to rank the following 11 features of a potential date by their importance in their decision whether to date them or not: character traits, job/income, looks, similar interests, similar dislikes, hobbies, lifestyle, similar world views, future plans, their habits and similar humor.

Most people said they were mostly or completely able to check these traits when meeting someone new, but a considerable amount of 24% stated they have problems to judge a person when first meeting them, a problem that might be solved by a more detailed communication in conversations and in online profile presentation.

The following traits are considered the top 5 of them for the majority of participants. Unsurprisingly more than half of students consider *character traits* their most important decision basis, with an average position (AP) of 2.7 (with a standard deviation (SD) of 2.9). However, 22,5% did not feature this criteria in their top 3 of 11 traits.
The second most important with an AP of 4.0 and one of the smallest SD's (2.1) appears to be *similar interests*. Almost 50% list this in their top 3, 80% in their top 5, but only 5% consider it their most important decision criteria.

Looks, which are used to match users in online dating, but also leave to first impression in real live, have only the third highest AP (4.6, SD 2.7), the same as a *similar humor*, on which, however, opinions vary more (SD 3.1). Both belong to the 5 most important traits to 2/3 of young people.

A person's *lifestyle* is averagely ranked in the middle (AP 5.9, SD 2.4), not being a lot of participants most or least important criteria. It is similar for *hobbies*, even if the persons asked seem to be even more agreeing on this, considering the comparably small SD of 2.1, being followed by *similar world views* (AP 6.4, SD 2.6)
Plans for the future are, probably due to the young age of the participants, not a particular important topic for almost 80% of them, who ranked it 6th place or lower, about 43% even only placed it in their "least 3". *Similar dislikes* play an even smaller part with similar ratings and an AP of 7.8.

There are great variances when it comes to deciding if the *job and/or income* of someone does influence if someone is willing to date them or not. It is the characteristic with the highest SD (3.3). Only 1/4 ranked it in their top 5.

More than half of all people consider *habits* of the potential partner to be one of the three least important considerations for their decision making, with about 57% it is the trait with the most "3 least important" rankings of all the traits.

feature / importance	character traits	job / income	looks	similar interests	similar dislikes	hobbies	lifestyle	similar world views	future plans	habits	similar humor
most important	55,0%	6,7%	9,2%	5,0%	1,7%	0,8%	2,5%	2,5%	1,7%	0,0%	15,0%
top 3	77,5%	16,6%	47,5%	46,7%	6,7%	7,5%	19,2%	15,0%	10,8%	7,5%	42,5%
first "half" (top 5)	85,8%	23,3%	65,0%	80,0%	12,3%	40,0%	42,5%	36,7%	21,7%	15,0%	66,7%
second "half" 6-11	13,3%	75,0%	35,0%	20,0%	87,7%	60,0%	57,5%	63,3%	78,3%	85,0%	33,3%
least 3	8,3%	55,0%	11,7%	4,2%	48,3%	15,8%	15,8%	22,5%	42,5%	56,7%	16,7%
least important	5,8%	30,8%	0,8%	0,8%	16,7%	1,7%	1,7%	3,3%	10,8%	16,7%	8,3%
ranked by	99,1%	98,3%	100,0%	100,0%	100,0%	100,0%	100,0%	100,0%	100,0%	100,0%	100,0%

	Feature	AP	SD
1.	Character Traits	2,68	2,89
2.	Similar Interests	4,04	2,07
3.	Looks	4,63	2,70
4.	Similar Humor	4,61	3,14
5.	Lifestyle	5,91	2,39
6.	Hobbies	6,23	2,07
7.	World Views	6,37	2,60
8.	Future Plans	7,45	2,62
9.	Dislikes	7,81	2,70
10.	Job/Income	7,90	3,31
11.	Habits	8,25	2,41

This shows that dating decisions of young people focus less on long term attributes and more on factors that determine experiences and fun together. But more importantly it demonstrates that sharing interests, even if only slightly, is considered more important in the dating decision than looks. People also seem to be more agreeing on it´s spot on the list, indicated by the lower standard deviation, so a stronger emphasis on getting to know the interest of the other person faster in online dating can be advised.

Furthermore, about 40% would be interested in basing the online dating experience on fandoms, allowing them to see a part of the others interest right on their profile Of the persons that already used online dating, it is even 58%

3.3.3) Usage of online dating services

While online dating portals, like the name implies, are mostly focused on relationships, young people use it for various porpoises. In fact, only 32% of them use it because they want to find a partner. What someone is looking for participating in online dating influences what kind of service this person will be drawn to and how satisfied the user will be with a certain service.

11

The most frequent use is actually *"just for fun"*, so to have some nice conversations, spend some time when bored etc., but with no goal concerning the establishment of a relationship of any kind. These people, understandably, prefer to exclusively use an app over using a website, probably because they are less invested and will rather use it in a free minute on the way than using it intensively on their PC. With being 36% of online dating users, this group should not be forgotten with designing or improving such a service.

People explicitly looking for a *romantic relationship* are the only of these groups which express any interest in using a website (21%) rather than an app or are willing to use both. A common complaint of members of this group is the number of fake profiles which makes a harder for them to get in touch with other people interested in the same thing, which might be one reason why less than half of these people were actually successful in finding a partner online so far. About 60% of them use online dating services that use more than just a picture for matching, even though this services mostly tend to have a smaller users base in not so big cities like Stralsund. Therefore, they are the group that can be targeted the easiest with innovations in the dating market.

There are also young people that do *casual dating*, a kind of dating where a relationship might be desirable but not the explicit goal. Those people, which are 20% of the target group, might be looking for sexual adventures or just a good talk where the outcome of meeting someone is unclear and less important than having a good time at the moment. There is a strong preference towards apps as well (over 50%).

The smallest of the groups with only 5% are people that use online dating as a mean to find *new friends*. These are surprisingly the users with the highest rate (60%) of having actually succeeded their quest and are more likely to know a huge amount (60%) of others that were successful in whatever they were looking for in the use of this service.

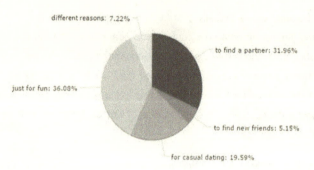

different reasons: 7.22%

to find a partner: 31.96%

just for fun: 36.08%

to find new friends: 5.15%

for casual dating: 19.59%

3.4) Personal Interests and Fandoms

Since shared interests are ranked the second most important trait to attract someone in this survey, it is only natural to take a look at what interests the target group has and how this affects their life.

When asked how much the own interests and fandoms affect their life on a scale from 1 to 10, 64% chose 1, 2 or 3, stating that it has an enormous impact on it. Only 15% selected a value lower than 5. The average value of 3.6 shows clearly that the young people asked are mostly willing and able to have their daily life and choices be influenced by things they like.

How much of an impact do your personal interests and fandoms have on your life?

Anzahl Teilnehmer: 110

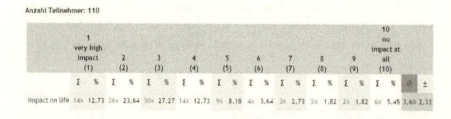

	1 very high impact (1)		2 (2)		3 (3)		4 (4)		5 (5)		6 (6)		7 (7)		8 (8)		9 (9)		10 no impact at all (10)		Ø	±
	Σ	%	Σ	%	Σ	%	Σ	%	Σ	%	Σ	%	Σ	%	Σ	%	Σ	%	Σ	%		
Impact on life	14x	12,73	26x	23,64	30x	27,27	14x	12,73	9x	8,18	4x	3,64	3x	2,73	2x	1,82	2x	1,82	6x	5,45	3,60	2,33

Therefore, sharing interests and fandoms with friends or the partner has scored only slightly lower results. While it seams more important that friends have the same interests, than that the partner does, both averages (3.9 friends, 4.2 partner) are quite similar. Even though a slightly higher percentage of participants ranked friends between 1 and 4, about 1.4 times as many people considered having the same

13

interests as their partner enormously important (rank 1), compared to interests of friends.

How important is it for you that your friends or your partner share your interests and fandoms?

Anzahl Teilnehmer: 112

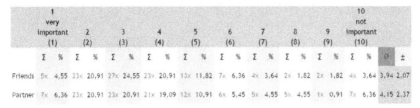

	1 very important (1)		2 (2)		3 (3)		4 (4)		5 (5)		6 (6)		7 (7)		8 (8)		9 (9)		10 not important (10)		Ø	±
	Σ	%	Σ	%	Σ	%	Σ	%	Σ	%	Σ	%	Σ	%	Σ	%	Σ	%	Σ	%		
Friends	5x	4,55	23x	20,91	27x	24,55	23x	20,91	13x	11,82	7x	6,36	4x	3,64	2x	1,82	2x	1,82	4x	3,64	3,94	2,07
Partner	7x	6,36	23x	20,91	23x	20,91	21x	19,09	12x	10,91	6x	5,45	5x	4,55	5x	4,55	1x	0,91	7x	6,36	4,15	2,37

Seeing that sharing interests is relevant for a high percentage of the young generation one might wonder what their interests are. The participants were given 18 fields of possible interests and were able to add own ones, to determine what they enjoy.

Rating the concepts from 1 (very interested) to 4 (no interest), the notions with the most common interest on average are:

listening to music (1.52; SD 0.75), *nature and outdoor activities* (1.75; SD 0.87), *cooking* (1.86; SD 0.89) and *movies* (1.97; SD 0.84). On average only 20% of people were not much or not at all interested in these activities. Combining this with the comparatively low standard deviations (average SD 0.96) there are good chances to meet someone who shares these interests, even when not particularly looking for it.

Anyway, it would be more complicated to find someone with the same interest when the person cares for *video games*. Even if it is not the field of interest with the fewest fans, it has the highest SD (1.18) of all the activities by far, showing that the participants are widely split on this activity, having 44% being interested in it.

The activities with the highest averages (over 3.0) and therefore the ones were finding someone with similar interests is the least likely are *anime and manga* (Japanese cartoons and comics) (3.54; SD 0.85), *programming* (3.4; SD 0.9), as well as *creating music* (3.08; SD 1.04) and *creative writing* (3.10; SD 1.0), which at least have an above average SD. These significant differences in interests might be a reason why 52% think that there are not sufficient possibilities to get in touch with fellow fans nearby. For people interested e.g. in programming these number is significantly higher with 68%.

The most common self-inserted answer is *travelling*, something 4% of participants immediately thought of when confronted with the topic of interests.

How interested are you in...

Anzahl Teilnehmer: 108

	very interested (1)		interested (2)		not much interested (3)		not interested (4)		Ø	±
	Σ	%	Σ	%	Σ	%	Σ	%		
movies	34x	31,48	48x	44,44	21x	19,44	5x	4,63	1,97	0,84
books (fiction)	21x	19,63	35x	32,71	29x	27,10	22x	20,56	2,49	1,03
books (non-fiction)	17x	15,89	41x	38,32	35x	32,71	14x	13,08	2,43	0,91
TV series	35x	32,71	40x	37,38	17x	15,89	15x	14,02	2,11	1,02
anime / manga	6x	5,66	7x	6,60	17x	16,04	76x	71,70	3,54	0,85
drawing or other creative output	10x	9,43	34x	32,08	25x	23,58	37x	34,91	2,84	1,02
creative writing	10x	9,43	18x	16,98	29x	27,36	49x	46,23	3,10	1,00
creating music	11x	10,38	20x	18,87	25x	23,58	50x	47,17	3,08	1,04
listening to music	65x	61,32	29x	27,36	10x	9,43	2x	1,89	1,52	0,75
watching sports	13x	12,15	19x	17,76	26x	24,30	49x	45,79	3,04	1,06
doing sports	35x	32,71	39x	36,45	18x	16,82	15x	14,02	2,12	1,03
celebrities	7x	6,54	30x	28,04	29x	27,10	41x	38,32	2,97	0,97
video games	22x	20,56	25x	23,36	19x	17,76	41x	38,32	2,74	1,18
programming	5x	4,67	15x	14,02	19x	17,76	68x	63,55	3,40	0,90
cooking	46x	42,99	35x	32,71	21x	19,63	5x	4,67	1,86	0,89
concerts	29x	27,10	45x	42,06	21x	19,63	12x	11,21	2,15	0,95
theatre	11x	10,38	40x	37,74	32x	30,19	23x	21,70	2,63	0,94
nature / outdoor activities	51x	48,11	35x	33,02	15x	14,15	5x	4,72	1,75	0,87
computer hardware	1x	100,00	-	-	-	-	-	-	1,00	0,00
cyclecross	-	-	-	-	1x	100,00	-	-	3,00	0,00
learning something new	1x	100,00	-	-	-	-	-	-	1,00	0,00
musicals	-	-	1x	100,00	-	-	-	-	2,00	0,00
Spending time with other people/frie...	1x	100,00	-	-	-	-	-	-	1,00	0,00
Travel	1x	100,00	-	-	-	-	-	-	1,00	0,00
travelling	3x	100,00	-	-	-	-	-	-	1,00	0,00

15

Different people express their interests in different ways. There are various fan activities one could take part in. The most common, and in the age of the Internet probably the easiest one, is just *staying informed* about whatever it is the person is a fan of, might it be new songs of an artist, upcoming events etc. 77% state that is way they express their fandom. With a long distance the next most popular way is going to *fan events, concerts and conventions* (41%), followed by an interest for *analysis and reviews* (31%). Also 28% of young people cheer for their favorite team or athlete.

Since the percentages of other activities are rather small, they will be showcased in this diagram.

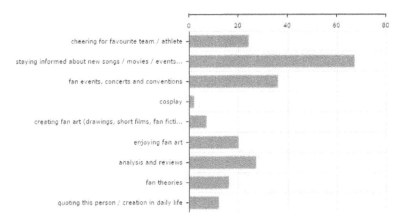

3.5) Interrelations

While this assignment focused on general findings up to now, there are different results for different groups of people and further correlations between the answers.

For example, female participants have slightly different expectations when dating than male. Their main focus is more often to find a partner when using online dating (34%), with the "just for fun"-use only ranked second. Even if fewer women than man have tried online dating, the women of this sample seem to be more successful with it than the men.

Women: 59% used, 26% succeeded,

Man: 64% used, 18% succeeded

They also claim that looks are less important for them than men do, giving it an average position of 5.3, while men place is 4.1. A more important aspect for them is a similar sense of humor (4.0; compared to 5.8). Also, they seem to value sharing interests with friends and their partner more.

Since it has already been established that there are interest groups less common than others, it is only appropriate to observe if answers from less average interest groups vary from the average. Even tough it might be pure coincidence and might differ in other samples, there are some findings that could be used in targeting and marketing to these groups.

Participants who are very interested in *anime or manga* almost exclusively use online dating to find a partner (only 1 differing answer) and 40% of them have already succeeded in this. They are more likely to talk to strangers to find a potential date than the average and consider themselves good at judging others when first meeting them. Their fandoms and interests have a higher impact on their life (2.7) and more of them enjoy fan art than the average person. There is also a higher interest in using a dating app based on fandoms (67%). A corresponding interest is playing video games, 83% of people who are very interested in anime chose the same option for video games as well. Using this information, it should be considered that these people are 67% male and are aged between 19 and 22.

Someone who spends their free time preferably by *programming* is likely to care more about the job, interests and dislikes of the potential partner than the average person, but less about their character traits and humor. 40% of them have tried online dating, exclusively to find a partner. In contrast to most participants, there is a significant number of people who would prefer online dating on a stand-alone website and no app preferences. 40% of them state that it is not easy for them to find out about other peoples traits when first meeting them, and even 75% think there are not sufficient possibilities to meet fellow fans. There seem to be connected disinterests in music and watching sports. 3/4 of this group are male.

The participants who much like to *create music* prefer casual dating (43%). Almost 1/3 struggles to check the traits of new people. They are more invested in analysis and reviews (18%) and generally base their life more on what they are interested in or fan of (2.5) than the average person. This group, consisting to 72% of men, also mostly enjoys concerts (1+2: 100%) and theatre (1+2: 64%).

Creators of writing seem to value character traits, humor, future plan and world views more than the average, however, care less about looks and similar dislikes. Fandoms and Interests have more impact on their life (2.8) and they also quote creations and persons they like more often in their daily life (44%). This 78% female group often enjoy other creative outputs like drawing, as well as nature and movies.

3.6) Conclusion for the online dating market

3.6.1) Development of niche market

To prove that there is a strong potential in online dating based on fandoms and other significant interests, one might not only look at the absolute figures, but show what kind of people belong to the potential costumers.

While the proportion of 40% interest in using a fandom based online dating service seems promising, but even more convincing seems that 12.5% of people who never used online dating before would be willing to give that a try, improving the costumer base of online dating as a whole.

There is a strong preference for app-only use. (41%). The interested people use, much like the average, online dating mostly just for fun (39%) and to find a partner (36%), which secures one target group that would use the service for a longer period of time and one that might leave after succeeding, but before that, spend a longer amount of time on the app and might return later on, if pleased with the service.

While the traits that they value the most are close to the average, 29% state that they do not think it is easy checking these, so it might be useful to implement voluntary information about hobbies, personality traits the like about themselves etc. on the profiles, as well as maybe short personality tests.

Potential users show above average interests in the general fields of movies, fictional literature, TV shows, creative writing, celebrities and video games, but also added hardware, travelling and learning something new to the list. When asked about their fandoms, 45% named a certain type of physical activity, including football (13%),

18

volleyball (6%) and dancing (6%) or sport in general. 1/4 named music, or a certain genre of it, to be one of their most important fields of interest. Of the 18 named fictional creations, including books, TV shows and movies, Harry Potter is the one with the most fans in our sample (19%), followed by the series Supernatural and Criminal Minds (both 6%).

People like to express their devotion about these and other fandoms more than the average as well, almost 90% are informed about new information concerning their fields of interest, while half of the fans join events like concerts and conventions. Over 1/3 also cheers for teams or athletes, plus as many people enjoy fan art. 11% even create fan art themselves. There are also values close to 30% for fan theories, reviews and inserting quotes into conversations.

Considering this, it might be worth a thought to include message boards, ways to personalize the profile or similar means to express their fandoms on the online dating portal, to make them log in more often and spend more time on it. Since the majority of over 60% thinks there are not sufficient possibilities to get to know fellow fans nearby, and some individual opinions were given that people are interested in getting to know people for other reasons than dating, this might improve this process.

Even if there is an interest in such kind of service, one of the most important aspects, especially in smaller towns, is the amount of people using the app nearby. Without offering users the possibility to meet other users that live in or around the same area, the market entering would changes from competing with general online dating to competing with creativity or information based fandom apps like Amino, Fandom powered by Wikia etc., as well as even Tumblr and Twitter, which is a much more saturated market and therefore harder to enter.

The fast spread of knowledge and use of the app would, on this account, be a pressing matter. The use of marketing methods, like trough social influencers, is therefore highly advised.

3.6.2.) Development of online dating in general

A frequently expressed wish of costumers, named in the open questions, is to focus less on looks and more on character. The often used limitation on the appearance of a person is described as "not very meaningful". It is even suggested once that the total opposite, so not seeing the potential partner, might be interesting. Since looks still are the third most decision criteria in our ranking, it is still an important aspect on choosing a partner and can not be ignored completely, but also cannot be the only information to offer to interested people.

Other aspects are not as clear and should be decided individually for each format. On one hand, users wish for less fake profiles, achieved by using social media profiles as verification or by making the service for paying costumers only. On the other hand, some are putt off by the need to link their dating profile with their social media accounts and / or are not willing to pay.

Another suggestion made by participants is a more specific matching algorithm, leaving it not only to the user to browse trough all the possible dates, but to make better suggestion about someone who could be a good match for them. This would also require more personal details that are relevant for the costumers.

While, with 5% of our participants, meeting new friends via online dating is a considerable small market by now, it is also suggested to have a "meeting app" as opposed to a pure dating app. This might pay off in a society that, especially in larger cities, becomes more distant and anonymous. However, for solid assumptions further testing would be needed.

To conclude, costumers would tend to be more loyal and probably spend more time in online dating platforms if they would expect a higher success and experienced a service that feels tailor made for their needs. A higher usage of existing costumers might be achieved by personality tests with porpoise of finding someone fitting to them, or games and quizzes to get to know the other. Possibilities of profile customization, in a visual and content orientated way may also lead to more usage and a higher identification with the service and the company behind it.

3.) Final Statement

While this report could be considered a proof of the hypothesizes made in the beginning, (There is a niche market for a fandom based dating apps.,
Users prefer character over looks and therefor want more possibilities to find out about it faster.), it is not an easy answer if acting on this assumptions would really be profitable. Existing methods and concepts have, even if often criticized, proofed to be successful and might attract a larger costumer base than new approaches. Still, if costumers get tired of the old methods, there is room for progress and it might be found in exactly the direction presented here.

4.) Appendix

5.1) Sources

Stewart, Caitlin.; 2016; MarketResearch.com
The Dating Services Industry in 2016 and Beyond, May 23, 2016
http://blog.marketresearch.com/dating-services-industry-in-2016-and-beyond

Statistic Online Dating, 2015, Statista
Statistiken zum Thema Online-Dating
https://de.statista.com/themen/885/online-dating/

Hochschule Stralsund, 2015
Entwicklung der Studentenzahlen
http://www.fh-stralsund.de/ueber-uns/hochschule/aktuelle-zahlen/Entwicklung-der-Studentenzahlen,navigation_id,245,artikel_id,80.html

Fryrear, Andrea; 2015, surveygizmo
Survey Response Rates, Jul 27, 2015
https://www.surveygizmo.com/survey-blog/survey-response-rates/

Anderson, Monica; Smith; Aaron; 2016
5 facts about online dating, FEBRUARY 29, 2016
http://www.pewresearch.org/fact-tank/2016/02/29/5-facts-about-online-dating/

Statistisches Jahrbuch 2015 der Hansestadt Stralsund
http://www.stralsund.de/export/sites/hst/buerger/rathaus/statistik/statistische_jahrbue
cher_gesamt/Statistische_Jahrbuecher_2008-2015/Statistisches-Jahrbuch-der-Hansestadt-Stralsund-2015.pdf

Lovoo, 2016
https://inside.lovoo.com/

N-TV, 2016
Die Verlockungen der Dating-App
www.n-tv.de/wissen/Fast-die-Haelfte-der-Tinder-Nutzer-ist-liiert-article16773976.html

OnlineConnections Inc., unknown year
http://www.onlineconnectionsinc.com/about.html

5.2) Graphics

All tables and graphics are created by the author
or are autocreated by umfrageonline.com to be used by the author.

5.3) Further remarks

- A collection of answers and evaluations can be found at:
  https://www.umfrageonline.com/results/ofd1jm-36e01d0

22